CITY to SURF

GORDON WINCH

illustrated by Shirley Blake

GINN

Contents

Chapter One

Out again

Lunchtime.
The usual din.
Kids running everywhere.
Howls of pain. Shouts. Laughter.
And down near the fence, the cricket match.
"You're in, Jake."
"Your bat, mate."
"C'mon, Jake."

Jake McLean pushed his glasses back on his nose and walked to the wicket. He picked up the old bat and faced Snotty Jackson who was bowling. There was a lump in his throat.

Snotty glared at Jake, took a long run, right back to the peppercorn tree, and tore down to the bowling crease. Snotty was fast — the fastest kid in Year 6.

"Why did I have to meet him?" Jake thought. "Bad luck."

With a loud grunt Snotty let the ball fly. It landed halfway down the dusty pitch.

Jake took a swing — and missed.

Clang!

The sound was crisp, clear and unmistakeable. The ball had hit the old garbage tin the children used for a wicket.
Jake was out.
Out for a duck.
Again.

He walked back to the playground seat with his head down. Slowly.

"Got ya, Four Eyes," said Snotty. "You're easy."

Snotty Jackson was Jake's arch enemy. He was big, chunky and strong as a bull. What's more, he had a loud mouth which he used a lot. And he used it to hammer Jake every time he could.

Jake had said nothing as he left the wicket. For one thing he couldn't think of anything to say; for another, Snotty was right. Jake was easy when it came to cricket. He just couldn't focus his eyes on the fast-moving ball.

What was worse he was "easy" at football, too. He always dropped the passes. And at basketball, he always missed the basket. And as for baseball — he hadn't managed to get to first base yet.

But what really hurt him was the way Snotty always jeered at him when he failed. It really hurt. Deep down.

One day he'd show that creep.

One day.

Some way.

All afternoon in school Jake was very quiet, very depressed. When the bell went he picked up his school bag and walked home — by himself.

Chapter Two

What to do

"It's no good, Mum, I just can't play," Jake told his mother.

"I've tried everything. I just can't play."

Kit McLean made some comforting noises. She said things about Jake getting better when he stopped growing so fast, that it didn't matter if he wasn't good at cricket and so on.

It didn't cheer Jake up a bit.

"You always say that, Mum," he said.

But in his heart he knew that his mother was trying to help, and he was glad he had her to talk to.

Jake's eyes had always been a worry. His new glasses made things a bit better. He could read really well now. The old problem still remained, though — he couldn't see the cricket ball when Snotty Jackson put a fast one down.

Jake was very tall for his age — he looked over the heads of most children in Year 6 — and he had long, skinny legs. Most kids called him Splinter. He liked that. Splinters were thin and long, but they were also tough — and sharp — and hard. Snotty Jackson was the only one to call him Four Eyes. If he could only show Snotty that he was tough and sharp and hard.

When his dad came home from work Jake was feeling a bit better.

"Want to come for a jog, Jako?" Mike McLean asked. "We'll take old Ben and run through the bush."

"Okay," said Jake.

"I'll tell you what, Kit," Mike McLean said later. "Old Jake's not bad on the hoof. He's really improved. He's got a good stride. And look at him after that long run — not even puffed. I think he's a bit of a natural. Those long legs really help. Think I'll take him along to The Striders on Saturday morning."

Mike McLean ran with the Sturt Town Striders. He'd been a good athlete at high school and now ran every Saturday with the club. He had won a few trophies. Jake's mum kept them in the lounge room, on the sideboard.

Jake was proud of his dad and his running.

He liked to wait at the finishing line and shout, "Go, Macka, go!" as the other people did.

"How about a run with the Striders on Saturday, Jake?" Mike asked.

"Okay," said Jake.

Chapter Three

The fight

Next week things came to a head at school. Snotty went too far, even for gentle old Jake. On the way out to lunch, Snotty put out his foot and tripped the tall boy.

Jake fell flat on his face on the hard ground. His glasses flew off and disappeared under the playground seat.

Jake was furious.

He saw red.

There wasn't much else he could see without his glasses.

But he had a fair view of the cheeky, grinning face of Snotty Jackson, and took a mighty swing at it.

Snotty hadn't expected this. He caught the punch fair and square on his stubby nose and took his turn at lying flat on the ground.

In seconds he was on his feet and the two boys flew at one another like a couple of bantam roosters.

The noise from the other children was deafening. Nothing better than a bit of a punch-up to give the day a sparkle.

"Give it to him, Jake!" they all yelled.

"Hit him again!"

Snotty Jackson had more enemies than friends at Sturt Town Primary. Jake wasn't the only one who had felt the lash of Snotty's tongue.

Snotty was much more solid than Jake and the fight was starting to go in his favour. He had butted Jake in the middle with his thick head and had managed to follow up this attack with a solid punch to the chin.

Then — "Beep!" — a shrill whistle and onto the scene strode a very angry Mrs Williams, the school principal.

"To my office, the pair of you," she thundered. "I'll teach you to fight in this school!"

Snotty's nose had bled a bit and Jake's ear was swollen for a day or two. That made the damage about equal.

What was more important, however, was the new attitude to Jake McLean that seemed to spread through the school. This spectacled beanpole of a kid was no softie after all.

Even Snotty Jackson himself had kept his tongue still for a week or so. And there was no more tripping or jeering. All that remained was a cold stand-off between the boys — ice where there had been heat.

Detentions, letters home and other punishments followed. The blame for the battle was equally shared. This didn't seem fair to Jake but he didn't complain.

The general feeling among the children was that the fight was a draw as well. Each boy had given and taken about the same.

Chapter Four

The cross-country

The Sturt Town School cross-country was a favourite event. It was run on Friday and almost everyone wanted to go in it, even the third graders. Jake didn't expect to do very well, but he was going to try.

Mrs Williams wanted everyone to run. "The Sturt Town School cross-country is a character builder, boys and girls. I want to see you all run. If you have a broken leg, you can run with crutches," she said as a joke.

The kids were not all that interested in character building, but the race was fun. They looked forward to it every year. The track was quite hard, up and down hill, and about 7 kilometres long. Sturt Town was on the edge of the metropolitan area of the city and there were paddocks, creeks and rough rocky hills to cross.

The Mothers' Club always provided soft drinks and cut up oranges at the end of the race. That was something to look forward to.

This year there were some good runners in Year 6 and Jake thought he'd be happy just to finish. What happened was a real surprise — for Jake, more than anyone.

When the race started, Jake ran with the crowd but at the halfway mark he noticed that he had left most of the school behind. Ahead he could see some speedy sixth graders who had dashed out in front. Among them was Snotty Jackson.

With 2 kilometres left to go there were only about ten runners ahead of him; he had been passing them one after the other. Soon there was only Snotty Jackson.

With 100 metres left, the pace quickened.
Jake was closer to Snotty now and slowly
catching him. He saw the finishing tape and
the cheering crowd. He ran over the line.
Second. Snotty had won.

As the boys went forward to pick up their
ribbons, they looked at each other coldly.
Not a word was said.

Chapter Five

City to Surf training

"Guess what, Dad?" Jake said one morning.
"I've been picked to be in a school team for
the City to Surf race. It's the teams event for
under-twelves — mixed primary, they call it.
Sure hope we do all right. We've got two
teams. I'm running with Fiona Curtin and
Jamie Horton. Don't know the other team
yet."

Jake found out soon enough. Next day in fact. The other team was Snotty Jackson and two of his friends. They were the clear favourites.

Snotty was acting true to form.

"We'll beat those other mugs," he boasted. "Old Four Eyes won't go the distance, anyway. He's easy — a bit soft."

Jake was determined to go the distance. He was out to beat boasting Snotty Jackson, too — and show him for the last time that he was anything but soft.

"Tell us the best way to run the race, Dad! What are the tactics?" he asked Mike McLean.

Mike had run the race many times with his club. He had taken over the training of Jake's team.

"You need to run a couple of times a week with Jamie and Fiona," he said. "City to Surf is a really tough run. Some very steep parts. The idea is not to go out too fast at first. You need to save up a bit of energy for the finish. I'll be there at the start, anyway. I'll give you some more tips then."

The three children were excited about the race. The whole school was talking about it, too. When the other team boasted about how well they would do, Jake and his friends said nothing.

Snotty Jackson and his team laughed at the training Jake's team was doing. "If you're good like us, you don't need to train," Snotty said to the other sixth graders. "We've got natural talent. Only mugs train."

"He might find that it's a different story on the day," Mike McLean told the children. "You'll see plenty of people who haven't trained, sitting on the side of the road! Some people need ambulance help, too."

So the little team of three went running, just as Mike McLean told them. They were better each time they trained.

Chapter Six

The race — the start

It was cold on the morning of the race, but the sun was shining. The McLeans and the other families got up early, had a light breakfast and drove into town. The race would start at William Street in the city, near the museum which Jake had visited on a school excursion some time ago.

Jake and his friends had never seen so many people. They were all standing together in the street waiting for the start.

Jake's team had last minute advice from Mike.

"Keep together for the first bit. I don't want you to be trampled by the crowd. Then run at your own pace. It's fourteen kilometres, remember. I showed you on the map. And drink plenty of water. Have some at every drink station. Can you think of anything else?"

"Yes," said Fiona. "We've got to watch the distances at the sides of the road. And remember that there's another kilometre to go when we reach Bondi Beach."

"And watch out for Heartbreak Hill," Jamie added.

"That's it. See you at the finish," said Mike McLean.

"Okay," said Jake.

The time for the start was getting near. The crane — the cherry picker Mike called it — had swung the officials above the crowd.

Then the voice of the starter could be heard.

"Good morning, everyone. Have a good race and enjoy the event. Good luck!"

Bang!

The starter's gun.
They were off.

Chapter Seven

Heartbreak Hill

The first part of the race was a blur to Jake.

All those people.

Shuffle, and jog.

Down William Street and up to the tunnel at Kings Cross.

Crowd starting to thin.

Puff, puff.

Jamie and Fiona not far away.
Now longer strides.
Longer strides.
Second wind.
Cruising along now.
Jake started to enjoy the race.
He remembered his training — not too
fast; steady pace; rhythm and even style.

Pat, pat, pat.

His running shoes tapped the road as he
ran along.

Then the drink station. Must get some water.

Sip! Swallow! Cough!

That's enough. Keep going!

Puff, puff!

The road began to climb sharply.

The runners began to slow.

Heartbreak Hill.

Jake shortened his stride and kept his rhythm.

He felt pain in his legs and his breath came faster.

"Got to remember how to do this," he thought. "Keep going. That's it. Steady does it."

He was glad of his training.

Many runners had slowed to a walk.

One man had stopped altogether.

But not Jake.

On and up he ran.

On and up and around the steep bend.

He couldn't see the others.

"I guess they're okay," he thought.

There it was. The top.

Some people in a garden beside the road were hosing the runners to cool them. Jake felt the welcome spray on his face.

"Thanks," he said and waved to them.

"Good on ya," yelled a little boy.

"Good on ya, mate."

Jake saw the 7-kilometre sign as he turned the corner.

He was nearly halfway and going well.

Could he keep it up?

Most of the runners had settled down to a steady pace. There were all kinds of people. A girl with a long ponytail passed Jake. Then he came to a man who was very old — and then a boy in a wheelchair. Jake felt proud to be in the race. He was going to finish, whatever happened.

Then he saw the two sixth graders in Snotty Jackson's team. They were not running very well. Jake passed them easily. He couldn't see Snotty though.

The next 3 kilometres seemed to last forever but then Jake saw the 10-kilometre mark and then the 11.

He was getting nearer to Bondi — and the finish.

The road began to level off.

Then it started to slope downward.

Jake felt his pace lengthen and his breathing was easier.

Then he saw the 12-kilometre mark. There were only two more kilometres to go now. Only two.

"C'mon, old legs," he said to himself. "C'mon ... Keep going ... Just a bit longer."

Then he had a big surprise. In front of him, looking very puffed, red in the face and hot was Snotty Jackson. He was barely moving and looked worn out.

When Snotty saw Jake, a defeated look appeared on his face. He slowed to a snail's pace. Jake shot past him and headed for Bondi Beach.

Jake had a new burst of energy and he ran on to the bottom of the hill. He had made it.

Chapter Eight

The finish

Jake turned the corner at the northern end of Bondi Beach and quickened his pace. Then he remembered, just in time. There was another kilometre to run. The length of the beach. He got back into stride and ran on.

Some people were finding the run too much. One man was being helped by the ambulance. Another man was walking.

But Jake ran on. It seemed forever.

"Go, Macka, go!"

"Go, Macka, go!"

There was no mistaking that sound.

Jake looked up and beside the road he saw his mum and dad waving and shouting to him.

"Go, Macka, go!"

He had a new burst of energy.

Jake waved to them.

There it was.

The last corner.

Down the hill he ran, through the
checkpoint to pick up his time.

He'd finished.

Some people were handing out oranges;
others were handing out drinks. Jake gulped
some water. Then he saw Fiona and Jamie.
They were just finishing, and they looked fit,
but tired.

The three children walked to the footbridge where they were to meet Mrs Williams and the other teachers who had come to see the finish.

"Good on you," they said.

About five minutes later, three more figures in school colours came over to the group.

They were Snotty Jackson and his team.

Snotty came over to Jake.

"Good run, Splinter," he said. "You beat us, fair and square. You're not easy. And you're not soft. You're hard. Hard as steel."

"Thanks," said Jake. And they shook hands.